Elegies
TO A DARK GODDESS

LINDA SANDEL PETTIT ED.D.

Ignite Your Magic
MEDIA

ELEGIES TO A DARK GODDESS

Copyright © 2025 Linda Sandel Pettit Ed.D.

First Published 2025 in USA by Ignite Your Magic Media, LLC in partnership with IW Press Ltd

The author asserts their right to be identified as the author of this work.

Cover art by Renuka Susan O'Connell

Images sourced from istockphoto.com:
- mitay20 (illustrating *The Right to Be*)
- Mariia Klymenko (illustrating *Crazy Love*)
- Tanya Syrytsyna (illustrating *Messages from the Black Madonna*)
- kiyanochka (illustrating *Yearning*)
- taylan_ozgur (illustrating *Mystery*)

Cover graphic design: 1981D
Interior design: Chapter One Book Production

All rights reserved.

No part of this publication may be reproduced, stored or transmitted without the express permission, in writing, from the author.

Library of Congress Control Number: 2025913875

A catalog record for this book will be available from the Library of Congress.

ISBN-13: 979-8-9992796-0-6 (Paperback)
ISBN-13: 979-8-9992796-1-3 (Hardback)
ISBN-13: 979-8-9992796-2-0 (e-book)

Ignite Your Magic Media, LLC. 101 W Seldon Ln, Phoenix AZ 85021
IW Press Ltd, 62-64 Market Street, Ashby de la Zouch, LE65 1AN

Love for *Elegies to a Dark Goddess*

"Dr. Linda Sandel Pettit's poems open a door to not only healing but understanding. Her message of divine love is heart saving for anyone at any stage of life."
—Patsy Kisner, Appalachian Poet,
Author of *Until the Surface Breaks*, USA

"Reading *Elegies to a Dark Goddess* was like stepping into a cathedral carved from the raw, holy places of a woman's soul. As an artist, I felt the rhythm of my paintbrush and pulse in every word. As a coach, I heard the echo of transformation in the ache and the rising. And as a woman, alive, loving, mothering, longing, I saw myself. Linda writes with luminous vulnerability and fierce grace. Her elegies are not just poems, they are initiations. This book met me in places I once thought too broken to revisit. It reminded me that beauty lives—even there. It is more than poetry, it is medicine."
—Terri Broughton, Artist, Coach,
Secondary School Headteacher (retired), UK
https://terribroughtonart.co.uk/

"I dare you to read *Elegies to a Dark Goddess* without tears and smiles as constant companions—I could not."
—Georgia Bazin, Coach, Author of
Love Liberation and Libido, UK

"Each elegy is a stepping stone to the raw truth of who you really are and to a creative life that reflects your deepest self. These poems empower you to drop your fears and lack of self-acceptance and instead radiate the energy from the Black Madonna's gifts of self-love, creative courage, and the willingness to embrace all emotions as you pursue your unique dream of fulfillment. Linda has given you a priceless ticket so that you can ride your train of raw truth, discern its genius, and then behold your unique manifestations."

—Gail McMeekin, LICSW, Coach, Author of
The 12 Secrets of Highly Creative Women, USA
https://www.creativesuccess.com/

"Through Linda's lifelong relationship with the Black Madonna, I've witnessed her intimate presence as human being, woman, and spiritual scientist. Her language of liquid light wends its way through grief and wholeness, urging me to seek the Beloved within."

—Renuka Susan O'Connell, Poet, Artist,
Author of *Cosmic Collect Call*, USA

"Novelist Hermann Hesse describes Rilke as evolving into his best poetry with the *Duino Elegies*, where *"at each stage now and again the miracle occurs, his delicate, anxiety-prone person withdraws, and through him resounds the music of the universe; like the basin of a fountain, he becomes at once instrument and ear."* Linda shows us her ability to be "at once instrument and ear," both comforter and comforted in her *Elegies to a Dark Goddess*. Through facing her own grief, she cries tears for all who have ever lost but wanted *"immunity from life's assaults."*

—Sarah Hook-Nilsson, Author of *Holy Days: Reflections of a Travel Pilgrim*, CA

"Immersed in this poetry to the soul, in the visceral images and potent prose, I found hidden depths of my being that melted sharp edges of my fifty-year-old's existential crisis. Through her depictions of the Black Madonna, I saw the contortions I embody when I only offer a protective motherly love—a fearful caring love that betrays the potential of my teenage children, my friends, family and myself, that I innocently dish out to give comfort and solace to soothe the 'terror of the abyss' but which actually comes at the cost of dulling the 'brilliance of the heart' and the channeling of love through us all."
—Kirstien Bjerregaard, Coach, Psychologist, UK
https://field-of-possibility.org

"Linda's poetry blew my mind and unraveled the protective wraps around my feminine soul. I fused into the beauty of the Divine Feminine. Holy innocence, lush with life. To read and read again."
—Anni Silverdale Poole, Psychospiritual Coach, Shaman, Author of *Simply Being You*, UK, https://annipoole.com

"Linda is one of those rare people who can see the tragedy and the beauty of life in equal measures. She pushes us to the extremes of both and encourages the reader to embrace it all if we are to truly live, evolve and experience Life at its richest depths. Her *Elegies* liberate as she expresses emotions many will not have articulated before and her quest and knowledge of the Divine Feminine inspire, guide and bring peace to the Soul. Linda Pettit stands raw and naked to give us a roadmap through Life and creative expression. Woven throughout with grace, courage, wisdom and fierce vulnerability, these *Elegies* offer rare insight into what it means to live a truly conscious life."
—Susie Spens, Homeopath, Writer, Coach, UK
https://susiespens.com

"Linda takes us on a journey through the dark doorway of our soul into rooms many of us fear to look, but ones that hold incredible light and unique gifts for powerful transformation. A brave and powerful sharing from the heart that holds the potential for deep healing and a new lightness of being."

—Bev Willcocks, Mentor, Artist, Mauritius

Dedicated to Laura

I love you forever.

I am the Divine Feminine, the Ground of Being.

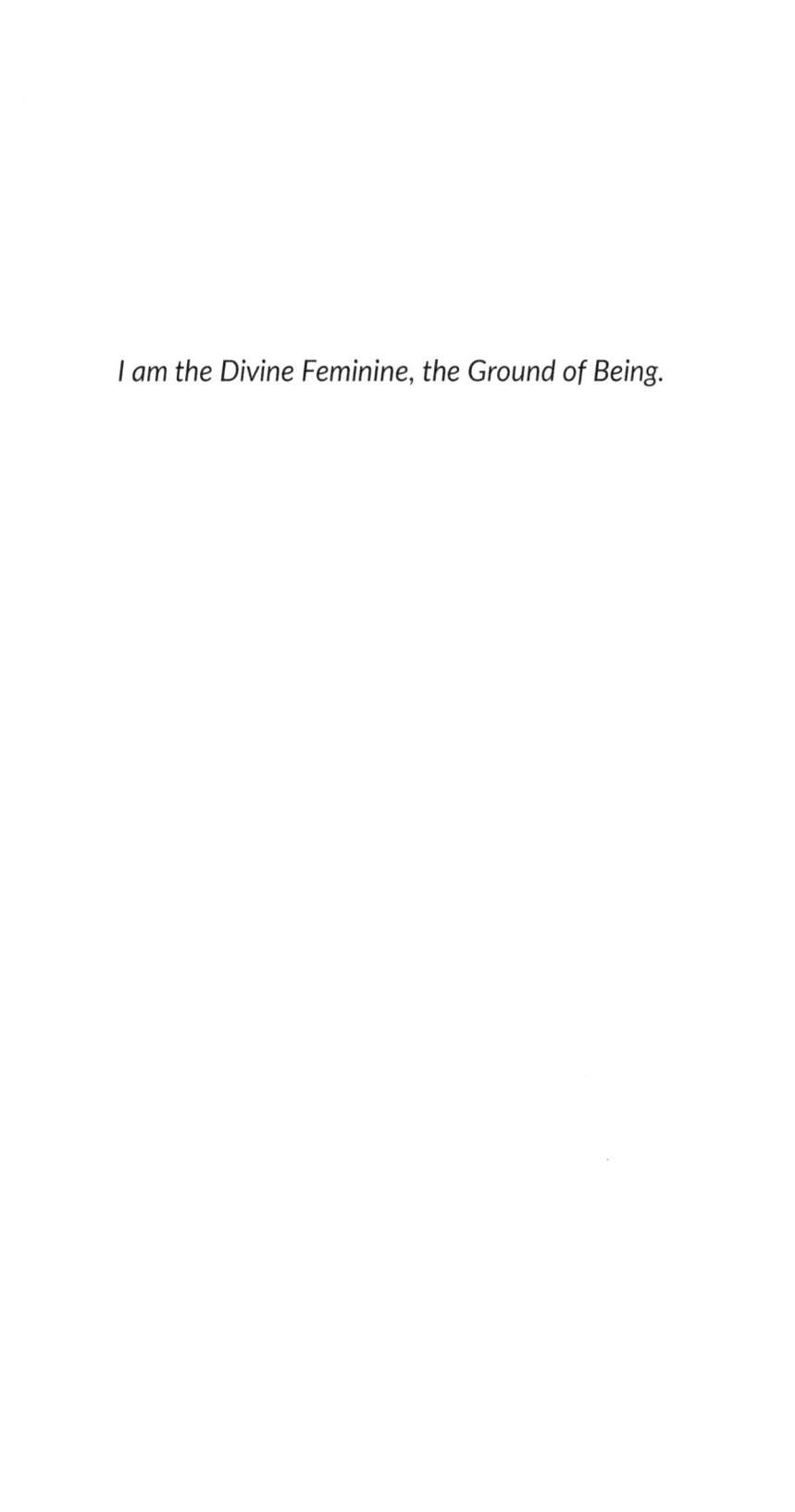

I am Listening and Stillness.

I am BEAUTY, creating.

I am the Divine Word, holy, good, and beautiful.

I surpass every constellation of the stars and shower the universe with Light.

I am She who heals; I am pure Love.

Contents

Prologue	1
Message from the Black Madonna	5
Initiation	7
Free Will	11
Crazy Love	15
Grief	19
Shadow Theater	23
Sprinkler Dance	27
The Right to Be	31
Mystery	35
Eve's Bite	39
Yearning	43
Epilogue	47
Connect with Linda Sandel Pettit	53
About the Author	55
Other Books Featuring Linda's Writing	57
Acknowledgements	59
Book Circle Questions	61

Prologue

> *"In the end, my choice, all choice*
> *is written as a victory for love."*
> —Linda Sandel Pettit

"I am NOT a poet!"
How often had I said that to my writing teacher, Jules Swales?

So, when she suggested I create my own version of Rainer Maria Rilke's *Duino Elegies*, I thought, *Too hard*.

I was even more reluctant when I realized the *Duino Elegies* were lamentations, reflections on grief, sorrow, and life's existential questions. That was territory I had no desire to revisit.

Like every human being, I have met sorrow in moments of shattered innocence. Disappointment. Tragedy. Betrayal. Heartbreak. I have also had to face and forgive my own behavior as the disappointer, the betrayer and the deliverer of wounds.

Yet, it was often in those passages through suffering and grief, those dark nights of the soul and facing myself, that I most felt the touch of a formless presence: a healer, a comforter, a meaning-maker. **She came not with** platitudes, but with a lamp lit by fire from the underworld, the place of alchemic transformation.

I cried a river of grief after my first husband, Jim, died in a car accident when I was forty-six. In time, the tragedy of his death brought me face-to-face with both the fragile beauty of human life and its stunning potential. During that transformative journey, the formless healer and meaning-maker—the Black Madonna, the Dark Goddess—took clearer shape in my heart and in my mind's eye. She would teach me that a heart broken wide can find heaven on earth in everything.

She is the womb where light embodies.
She is the essence and crucible of creativity.
She is the disruptor. She is the earthquake of transformation.
She is the mystery we meet when we join her.
She is the mother of all thresholds. She stands at the gates between what was and what might be, inviting us to shed our skin. She is snake medicine; she bites to awaken us to our infinite love, creativity and power.

The dense, layered language of Rilke's *Duino Elegies* was mysterious, often difficult to understand. Yet, when I listened to their deep feeling and wrote from that place, I unearthed an inner poet with much to say. Emulating *Duino Elegies* gave me words for sharing potent emotions and rich, big questions.

Through metaphors, I explored the mysteries of life and death.
Through symbols, I wrote my own version of sacred scripture.

I preface *Elegies to a Dark Goddess* with another, earlier piece I wrote years ago: *Prayers to the Black Madonna*. That piece hinted at the great healing that writing the *Elegies* would one day initiate.

While this is a book of poems, it is more than that. It is a testament to the healing potency of creative self-expression. It is a living witness to the love that emerges when we honor our wild voices, however they choose to speak.

This is spell work. This is alchemy. This is the truth of a woman who discovered she was always, already, an artist of life.

"Write from the soul. Light a fire in the underworld and dare to dance with it. That is how you remember you are a miracle—magic itself."
—The Dark Goddess

Message from the Black Madonna

Three Black Madonnas inhabit my office. One, with haunted brown eyes, looks at me from a small plaque hanging on the wall above my computer. I made a pilgrimage to a monastery in Częstochowa, Poland for her.

A second Black Madonna sits on my desk. A tiny statue made from wood, the shade of burnt sienna, I purchased her at a mountain top shrine in Montserrat, in Catalonia, Spain.

A third Madonna, an enigmatic silver sylph haloed in gold, watches from the wall above my copper water fountain. I drove fourteen miles down a rutted desert road in New Mexico to discover her at a cloistered monastery.

After my first husband's death, I was lost. Bereft. Blindsided. Unmoored. Empty.

The Black Madonna, the goddess of transformation, drew me close then. I huddled in her womb.

That was a tough time when a boulder of sorrow changed into gold through the alchemy of grief.

"Why did everything fall apart?" I asked. An indigo rosary draped the edge of my computer screen.

"No reason you'll understand," said the Black Madonna. I contemplated an incomprehensible world. Tears smarted like acid.

The Madonna whispered:

"This is the time of Great Disruption," she said. *"After will come the time of Great Reckoning. Only then, will come the time of Great Healing."*

Initiation

I am the Dark Goddess,
the Black Madonna,
to whom you descended.
No angels hovered in my chilly cave.

The abyss evacuated the marrow
from your spongy bones
and spit you out,
an innocent spineless skin,
a seeping organ of despair,
a pitiful child.

I stood impassive
to your shivers,
to keening cries,
to the battalions of anxiety
that marched inside you.
Entreaties for mercy
bounced off deaf walls,
feeble insults to the inevitable.

You wanted immunity.
from Life's assaults.
But I knew,
every delay suspended you
in a world of make-believe,
a world of stunted consciousness.

Your initiation to harsh reality
hid a boon,
a gem,
a diamond,
the brilliance of *seeing*,
the brilliance of *hearing*,
the brilliance of *knowing*,
the brilliance of *Love*.

Lament: your cries scored my heart,
Lament: your moans crushed my spirit,
Lament: your curses bruised my tenderness.
Lament: your tears eviscerated my eternal soul.

I yearned to give comfort.
Yet, aid would have betrayed you.
The Black Madonna I stood,
a stoic mother,
while the rage of a river,
a roiling current,
carved interiority with the weapon of death.

It's harder to move through life
without a darkened eye.
You would have emerged from the cave
blinded by the light,
rather than one with the light.

If you thought the terror of the abyss
was more egregious than
the terror of a sleeping heart,
a heart unable to find brilliance
in the obsidian night of the soul,
you were mistaken.

Hence: regret not initiation,
promised ecstasy in the fulfillment of fate,
a sail set to the sparkling harbor of destiny,
a seal on a journey of meaning
to the heart of darkness.

When the curtain falls, I, the Black Madonna,
offer the comfort and nourishment
of a dark breast swollen with the milk of God.

One day when least expected,
you will awaken from dreamtime slumber
and look up to see my face.
My ebony skin glows.
My magnificent candle bounces fire into your eyes.
You will know
that I never left you.
We are forged and fused
in the inferno of unquenchable love.

Free Will

I was written, some say,
as the musk of ebony ink
on creamy parchment
bound in plum-colored leather,
pages edged with gold,
a book that rests
in shafts of sunlight
aswirl with dust motes
on a shelf heavy
with the library of knowledge.
It is up to me,
to read the signs, the omens,
that soften stumbles
on predestined paths.
In this alchemic tale, I am devoid of free will.
I do not know if this is so.
The wizened librarian keeps her counsel.

I prefer to think I am a slender thread,
a crimson filament held,
with a mere gram of touch,
in the hands of the Dark Mother.

Seated at a wooden loom,
she pumps the treadle,
releases me from the spindle,
a warp in a pattern of beauty,
a masterpiece of her indrawn breath,
that is known only as she exhales.
Tilted to the light in ecstasy,
her tapestry is revealed
in the now of the Mind's eye.

I am a thread invisible to the eye, unimportant,
yet without my crimson note,
the masterpiece is a mountain without a sunset.
It is my free will to follow the direction
of the weaver's touch
or, to break her pattern.
In the end, my choice, all choice
is written as a victory for Love.

I reflect on my virginity, lost in service to Aphrodite,
that blood red fiber broke,
a velvet snap as the crescent hymen
tore open the gate of womanhood.
I surrendered with tender, naïve love,
given freely,
without asking the right questions,
and was betrayed.

Do I ever know another's heart?
I was a secret sarcasm,
shared among hot young warriors.
Betrayal revealed me, discarded, invisible.

I plunged into the abyss,
a second such descent,
this one an eternity in the night of Being.
I cannot accept this as pre-written.

No, the Dark Mother paused at Her loom,
as any Madonna would,
head bent to breast in sorrow.
And tying my slender silken thread
in a jilted lover's knot,
buried it, unseen, in her pattern.

A tear seeped from her eye,
wandered from the river of Love
to mark the spot with tender grief.
After the time that must be sacrificed to such losses,
a tug on my thread shuttled a new pattern.
I felt the Madonna's unseen touch
and could not but surrender to the confident artist.

The slender thread of my warp emerged,
an exploded star, a black hole,
a magnet for light to serve my destiny,
a wounded healer.
Written or co-created?
I know not.

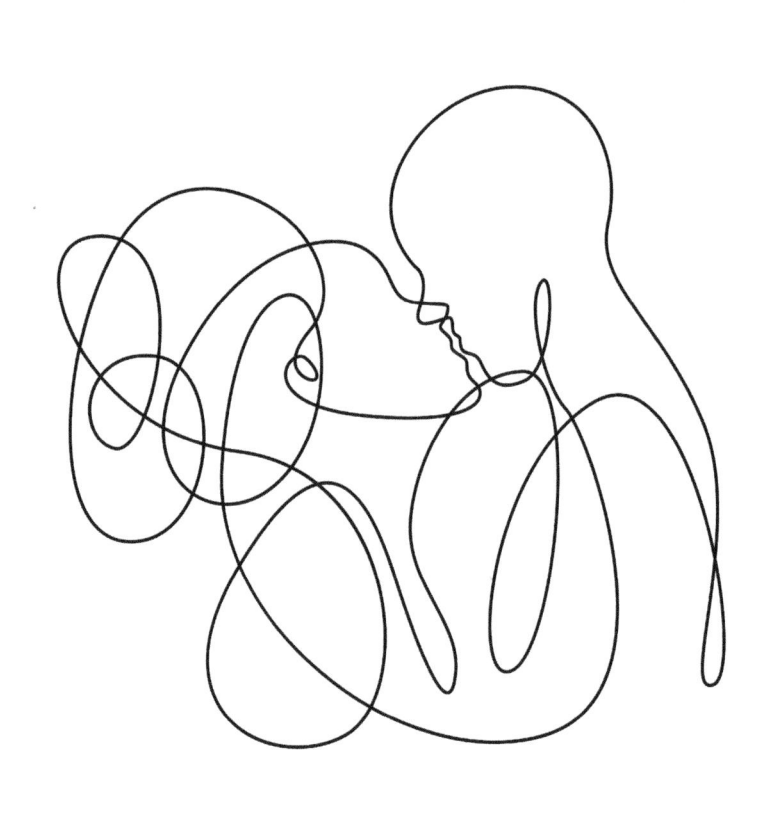

Crazy Love

A river
sourced in the inscrutable sea
of silent eternity,
cooled
in the dance of molecules,
leached whiffs of gas.
Life from placid bedrock.
Crazy Love.

Surrendered
by the watery bosom
of a dreaming sea,
overflowed bounty,
a landward tributary,
a river.
I am the Scorpion's sting.
Water sign fixed to Earth,
beholden to Air.
Fire hidden.

Trickling over mudded beds,
polishing speckled stones,
carving banks of soft edges.
I, a ribbon,
meandered into a story,
drawn by gravity,
a babbling tongue of separate Truth.

Sweet mother.
Why impregnate?

You knew,
Lady Madonna
you cursed the river
with the force of Love.
The year of the snake marked
my chrism,
even as the waters of baptism
offered salvation.
Crazy Love.

Why have a child?
Birth certificates are death sentences.
Signed, sealed, delivered.
In between, a river,
I must roll, must roll, must roll
beneath nights of fire,
a dispassionate moon
and hot stars that blink not,
unmoved by the drum of flumes.
Crazy Love.

A virgin river, unprepared
to engorge with rain,
to snarl with thunder,
to dash droplets,
to mizzle against unmoved boulders.
A break of current crushed
by the sweat and moan of libido.
Crazy Love.

Mocked futility.
The river encircled
the island of a priest,
a shaman lover,
devoted to Gaia,
who surfed
on a turtle shell
under bowed willows
to stay afloat
in swift currents
of libidinal urgency.
Crazy Love.

Mountains of foggy twigs,
ice dropping from a white sky,
blackened fate on a country road.
A guard-rail sprung the death trap,
snagged the float of kindness
from the river,
snatched the blink of Christmas,
and buried it on a ridge.
Divine destiny.
Crazy Love.

A coffin rests,
under the sycamores,
out of reach.
I roll still.
The Monongahela
river of fallen banks,
every day farther
from the dreaming sea.
One day a lost creek
will dry to land
and slip the curse, of
Crazy Love.

Grief

A phone's shriek, a herald's warble.
Christmas split in two: before and after.
Death stuck her nose in earthly business
and ignored the entreaty to stay in her lane.
How dare she?

Before: a mom, a dad, a daughter, a family.
An oasis crooked into the Great Mother's arms,
a crucible of learning, love bounded by edges.
Fragile certainty, pock-marked with suffering,
the misery of security.

After: angels unmoored, two souls
free-falling, a chasm of grief, desperate to hear
the song of the just dead. Left behind
to wonder, to wander, to burn tender feet
in the music of misery.

If you have not walked grief's hot coals
do not pretend to understand.
Save platitudes for trifles —
fictitious theater, tragic novels —
mere shadows to the undoing
of the real deal.

The angel of darkness
sucked an ocean of tears
into her black hole,
the mouth of mystery,
and spilled them, a deluge of mourning
onto the face of innocence.
She seized a glowing brand
to scorch her mark
on empty tear ducts.

The just dead.
Do they walk into Lament's garden,
discard lovers and children like crumpled leaves
on the Tree of Life?
Do they pivot
to a full illumination of the dream
forgetting the song
on the tip of the tongue?

Is there even a moment, a fragment of now
where they reach, heartbroken,
for the anchors that tethered them
to a spinning Earth?
Is there so much as a flash of sorrow
wrapped around bereavement's heart
in eternal solace?

Beyond these questions,
a knowing, an acknowledgement.

In the book of the dead,
the coupling of souls is recorded
in luminous ink,
a brilliant signature
on a dark page,
a star of hope, a radiant eternity.

Two or more gathered, there She is.

Shadow Theater

Contemplate dark mysteries
and layered dreams.
Consigned, I am, to decode
life through a rearview mirror.
Even then, to suffer
the deception of thought.
Consider shadow theater,
figments of divine dreams
on screens of flesh.

My lover encountered shadow puppets,
on the burnt sands of Malaysian beaches.
He met them in the barrios of Mindanao,
flickered light from coconut candles,
flat leather cut-outs raised on sticks by a puppeteer,
projected from behind
onto the hoi polloi's screen,
a sheet washed in the river of life.
Beyond, the watchers.

He loved shadow theater,
felt himself the Light,
the one-dimensional figurine,
the echo of shadow
and the observer.

He left a blue ceramic jar,
a fragile thing
to hold big questions
written in pencil
on a stenographer's notepad.
Follow an old pledge or make a new?
Live out destiny or create a fated end?
Live like a flat myth anointed with holy chrism,
sealed in a golden monstrance,
paraded in High Masses on altars of martyrs?
Or live another flat myth,
maleness thrust into turgid caves,
surged into orgasmic explosions,
trapped in the low masses
with the grunge of dirty diapers.
Either way, he chose Life.

I remember the day he held our daughter.
knew in her conception that he
had sealed her fate, bound her to
an ancient heart and accidental destiny,
a doll puppet he held up
onto the stage for such a slip of time.

He wandered and looked for the
perfect present to welcome her,
to beg her forgiveness,
to say hello and goodbye at the same time,
to thank her for making him whole.
He returned with a flimsy pennant,
a rainbow flag embossed with
hearts and her name.
He watched with love-blinded eyes
as her shadow moved onto the screen.

Was she the light, the leather cut-out,
the puppeteer or the watcher?
Was she all? He did not know or care.
His eyes beheld only Love.

I challenge you.
Tell me. Are we but shadows?
Brief figments of time? Fleeting projections?
Cut-outs hoisted on a screen.
Dolls, playthings of God
who pleasure the Divine appetite of consciousness?
I answer. Yes, I answer.
I answer, yes.

Yet in the silence,
I know
I observe the delusion
or the illusion
of shadowed theater.

Sprinkler Dance

Sun-kissed droplets, prisms of hope
arced in joy, bent with gravity,
beckoned a boy of laughter,
beckoned a woman shackled,
beckoned separate costumes.
Fusion masked, fission,
to step into delight's fountain.

Ice licked burnt skin.
Stung eyes shut to water.
All that was human cried halt! Stop!
Was the run of mascara,
the ruin of a dress
and matted hair, a fair price for
a ticket to the sprinkler's dance?

Why was he born? What boon did he bring?
This angel of light, Skywalker's comet,
Master Jedi, a galaxy's mystery.
Babe in a diaper, perfect fit,
innocent, unblemished, whole.
Face beloved by Grammy.
Fair Linda waited, wrinkled.

If I stepped into the fountain, could I
teach him that he was born to dare?
Teach him that light isn't so until it pierces
darkness. Teach him to break free.
A laughable thought, the paradox.
He was the teacher.
I, the primer.

The end of the line loomed.
Hand outstretched to help.
Responsible. Conscientious. Giving.
Creating. Expressing. Gabriel's angel.
Nothing mattered. Nothing counted.
Except, the decision.
Eschew caution, cascade life.

Beloved, I heard you sing
your backyard refrain.
Rankled sand in a bleached desert wind.
Do not think. Leap.
Leap!
Water tantalized
a heart into the Now.

Angel to joy
feathered light, he flew into wide arms,
buried head, supplicant neck.
Soul fused to mine,
whispered without sound
Grammy, you remembered
this reason, this Truth.

Toil in the field of purpose,
rapture in the field of dreams
seek the force field of an empowered mind.
You will not find treasure.
Strive not. See, in silence.
Go for the gold. Play.
Death depends on it.

Warm raspberries, savory Spanish rice.
Sweet apple juice in a sippy cup.
Vanilla bean ice cream with rainbow sprinkles.
Red, yellow, blue, and green sugar.
Ground wires needed.
Back to life. Back to form.
Melted into the sleep of naps.

This baby nestled into my weathered shoulder,
hand laid on hallowed ground
between shoulder and neck, sunken treasure.
Fingered clavicle, tickled hair on chin.
Sucked his treasured binky
Sandman's reward, a just sleep,
Grammy's salvation.

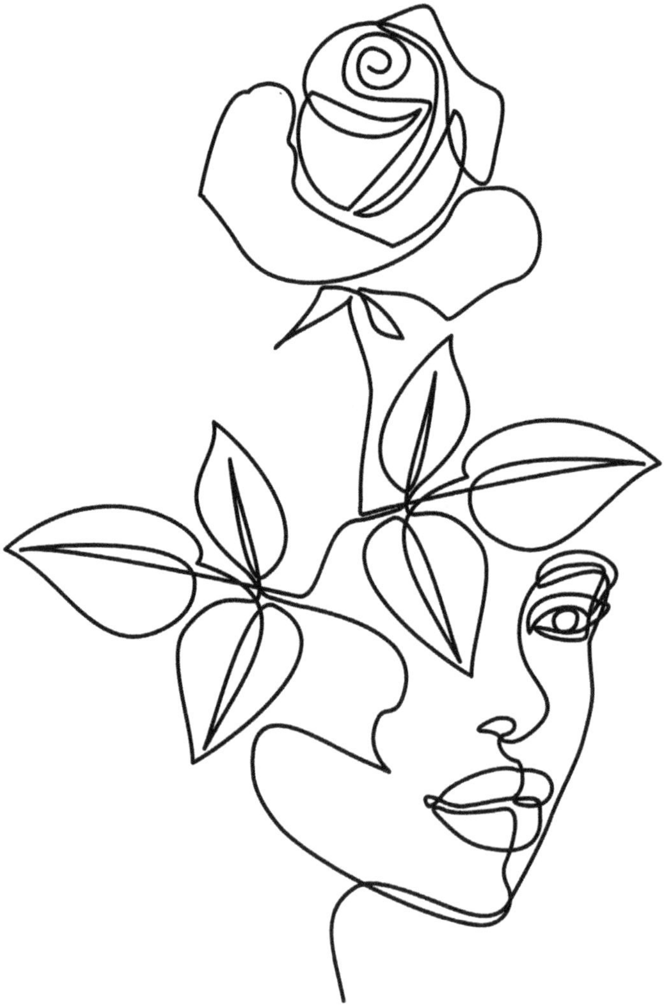

The Right to Be

Withered, parched fruit, life's last quartile.
Aches and pains assault unconscious slumber.
Swarthy marauders hack muscle and sinew,
eviscerate organs fragile, frayed with age.

Breasts surrendered to gravity, child long past fed.
Eyes dimmed; impressionism paints the world.
Parts missing, parts titanium,
every day a new cripple welcomed in the asylum.

I long, oh how I long, to curl into a rocking chair,
wave to palms that sway against cloudless skies,
rise to the erotica of the sun's fiery kiss on spotted skin,
inflate lungs with desert breezes, the breath of God.

Nothing to do. Nothing to think. Nothing but to relax.
Wait for death's scoop into heaven's magic.
The best, most free, most silent, most pregnant years
of a life brimmed with work and responsibility.

My fate is to be a fig, fruit that skipped the flower.
Flower of playfulness. Draught of rest.
Banquet of tropical holidays. Flower of meditation.
Sip of angel nectar. The lightness of being.
Beauty's flower.

A peace rose. White at heart, amity, and death.
Fringed yellow, hope and joy.
Tinged blush, innocent passion.
Urgent with life, trembling, sheer joy in bloom.

A peace rose. No reason but to exist
in showy beauty,
to delight passers-by
with noncontingent fragrance and loveliness.
Symbol of Truth, being in shadow and light.

A child stood under the kitchen window,
drank the elixir of mother's prize peace roses,
unaware the imprint of loveliness on optic nerves
reflected from the heart, the essence.

I earned the right to be
a peace rose.

Awards. Degrees. Jobs. Motherhood. Helping. Writing.
That, too. Writing as if life depended on self-expression.
Loving it all. And, oh, alongside the pace, a desire
to lay it all down in a bed of peace, rose of Being.

Too late, I wonder if there is another way to live.
To tip the balance, weight the scale toward rest
and yet fund this precious human existence.
Fund the right to stop, go slow, savor.

Another way to earn the right to be?

Jesus preferred Mary to Martha,
the sylph at his feet to the maid in the kitchen.
Loved the lilies of the field who neither toiled nor spun,
arrayed in glory. I missed the point.

Soft fruit, thin skin, a fig must earn its keep.
The cost of legitimacy a dogged pace,
a metronome of driven pressure,
seeded in separation.

Costumed in worry, the prize was spoiled.
The once and precious life spent in pursuit
of an Oscar for perfect spiritual theater.
No recording. An audience of one.

Exhausted. I am exhausted.
Too many musts, too much order.
Too many bees buzzing around compost,
nectar of helping funded with urgent despair.

I see no answer, no respite.
Rest is punctuation, not clause, lower case, not upper.
Plodding, a seventieth-year fruit, fig,
dreams of alchemy, a peace rose.

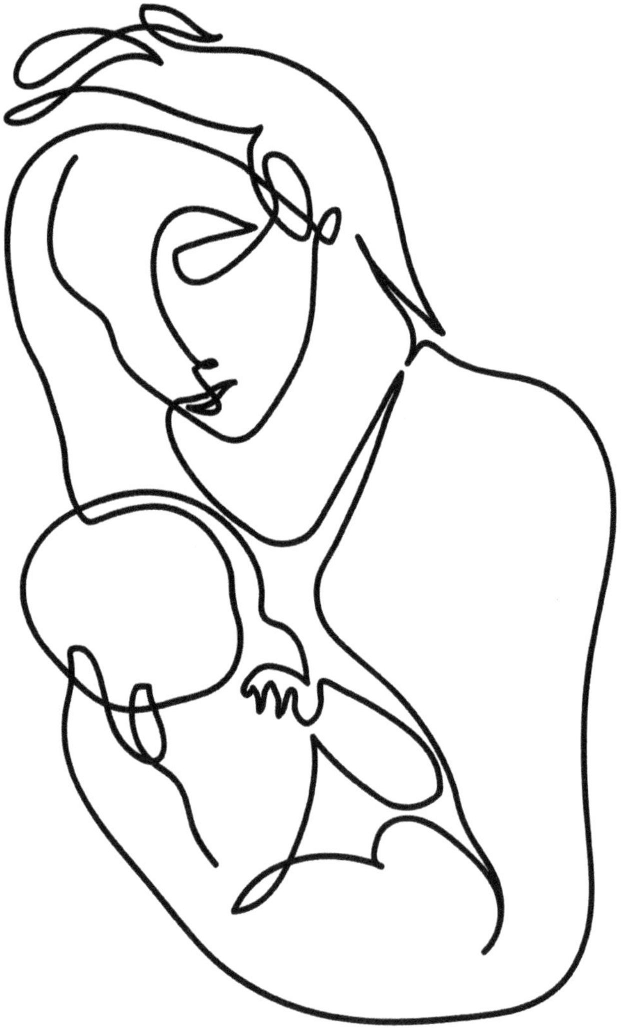

Mystery

O, sweet tiny embryo,
pure feeling, afloat in mother's sanctuary.
Do you know your Self?
Yet unformed cell of consciousness.
Yet inseparable flash of lightning in the eye of God.
Yet word. Yet thought. Yet pure love.
Enjoy these eternal moments of unfettered bliss.
Until irresistible forces compel the brightness of fate.

Blink, oh, blink in wonder. Blink in bewilderment.
Where am I? Who am I? What place is this?
Every thought, an innocent judgment.
I am warm. I am cold. I am wet. I am afraid. I am alone.
Every thought, a shadowy filter.
She is milk. She is here. She is not.
She is witch. She is Goddess.
Every thought, an experiment.
I am satisfied. I am not.
I am whole. I am not.
I am hated. I am not
I am loved.

Forming, forming, forming a prison of identity.
An innocent potter shapes a container
on the wheel of life.
The circle turns, turns, turns as the mold is formed.
Forever: an earthen vessel of size, shape, style.
Eternal: a pot to treasure dirt and seed.
Mystery: a pitcher engineered to pour water.
Magic: oh magic, now a creature with a name.

Unbridled joy gives way to shyness.
Arms stretched to the sun; a naked body covers itself.
Explorations become mischief.
Simple appreciation paints a canvas on the wrong wall.
Behavior, once innocent, assumes purpose.
Love once without boundaries, once so pure,
hides, begging to be seen, to be understood,
to be welcomed.

Does the eye of God blink in dismay, and
award only one star to ill-begotten spiritual theater?
Write judgment on the ledger of purgatory?
Hold its head in despair at exponential reproduction
of misguided unconscious acts?
A cancer of innocence, an unnatural tumor
in the superconscious.
Starving its host to freedom,
the creativity of angels and Divine Will.

Or does the eye of the Beloved simply behold?
The sweetness of benevolence, a practice of Kintsugi.
Rough edges smoothed with time's platinum.
Cracked fissures strengthened with the space of silver.
Broken places made beautiful with gold's filigree.

The Mind, the Master, seeing only
magnificence and majesty
in the perfect imperfection of a tiny creature's dream.

And we, we know not.
Bereft of our ageless memories across stages,
playgrounds, lives.
Guessing alone at the nature of our source,
consigned to wander the hall of mirrors,
holograms of time, space, and matter,
reflections of our wander, our wonder.
Guessing no self to know.
Guessing Self, we can never know.

Guessing, accepting, joining,
the mystery of not knowing.

Eve's Bite

The album I take with me to Death's door
is filled with treasured photos.
That picture of me, a pink-cheeked
toddler in a navy-blue bonnet, a thin
string tied under a neck
folded in chubby layers.

Oh, the one of a 10-year-old innocent,
a maiden with freckles marching across a pert nose.
The apple of her father's eye.

First wedding, the single day in seven decades
where I felt an uncommon beauty,
an angel radiant with love beyond understanding,
cloaked in an Alfred D'Angelo gown
studded with crystals.

A young mother, flower-speckled hospital gown
draped from her shoulder,
holding faith in life, faith in continuity,
faith in love, a daughter, a gift of all saints.
The apple of her father's eye.

The doctoral hood, blue and gold, a mantle
of intelligence slipped on slender, proud shoulders.
A license to practice listening, a life's passion.

Mountains, oh the majestic mountains.
The beloved tender mountains enveloped a quiet life
and entombed a dead husband.
Plaid-shirted bones stripped of flesh, held
in gold suspenders.
The apple of his father's eye.

A second wedding. A heart mended and regifted.
Another ivory gown, satin, a train of hope.
An intimate partner, light, and lens.

Five children, eleven grandchildren, three greats.
An elder on the desert of choices, stunted dreams,
gloried blooms.
Faded eyes, wrinkled arms, seventy rings of a tree
Yet alive, so alive, alive with images of possibility.
The apples of her eyes.

Oh, I cannot grapple such beauty be meaningless.
Why would a goddess not gather to her breast
every minute of sorrow, romance, labor, and joy?
Why would she not prize these with eternal appellation?
Indelible photos shrouded with meaning.
Enduring consciousness formed for eternity
Eve's bite of the apple, not the fall but the rise.

Cyborg words an insufficient metaphor for creation.
Man's girdle on the unsayable power of a heart
that breathes essence into purple violets,
the Pieta's sorrow,
the mist-shrouded miracle of the Gaspe's sweep,
poems of art, bodies of joy, feelings treasured.
captures of transience, faded paper, bytes on a drive.

Carried beyond the threshold?
Abandoned to the blink of a heart?
No eyes, no apples.

Yearning

Yearning no longer:
yearning will not quicken desire,
a dowager's folded treasure,
tissue-wrapped memorabilia,
layered into an oaken chest,
tightened by bands of brass,
shackled with a copper padlock,
dragged into dim recesses
of a capacious attic,
an ancient confessional,
the soul of the Goddess
her heart pierced by the ornate key.
Divinity's thorn.

Lured into darkened cathedrals,
dropped to its knees at golden altars,
yearning searched for poetic justice,
the absence of judgment.
A drop of water
sluicing down a bottomless well.
Spilling to no end,
no rest,
no merger into a pool of knowing,
no grail.

Lured into the arms of lovers,
knees opened to the thrust of life,
yearning arched toward ecstasy.
The climax was fleeting.
A burst of joy on the tongue
receded into effluvia,
swallowed in the march of time.

Lured by the promise of meaning,
yearning spent untold energy creating,
never enough.
Yearning broke the body,
chafed the spirit
lacerated the heart,
and pined, merciless.
Yearning barreled, a train unchecked,
steaming,
steaming,
steaming
toward disaster,
the doom of metallic wreckage.
Life a smoking mess
of splintered dreams,
shattered bones,
decimated flesh
and silent death,
the specter of nothingness.

Nowhere Beloved,
will satiation be found,
but within.
Only in the heart's cavern,
seen by no one,
celebrated by no one,
adored by no one.
The grail hides,
a tabernacle cloaked in invisibility.

Humble, as Francis's Portiuncula.
Unassuming, a fairies' spring
merged into a hillside canopied in forest,
carpeted with plumy ferns.
Without form, ethereal,
beyond the third eye's sight,
a door opens into mystic wonder,
a fire dances before the eye,
etches ashen traces of its existence,
then vanishes into the cool, good night.

The wisp of flame
ignites the soul's remembering.
Poets write,
dancers choreograph,
sculptors chisel,
painters brush,
in homage,
not yearning.

Forgetting,
the lapse into yearning,
is a strange thing.
Sleepwalkers bumble in shuttered attics,
dust burns noses,
sneezes shower particles of detritus
into the moted air,
shins bang against unseen furniture.
Wraiths search,
grasping,
grasping,
grasping,
for the sacred key.

Prodded by the tines of stars,
startled by the lanterns of angels,
puzzled somnambulants awaken,
genuflect, penitent,
and ascend,
one foot
and another
and another,
on the interior castle's stairs.
Avila's dream.

Yearn no more.

Epilogue

One of my aunties told this story about my maternal grandmother, Tillie—or Tekla—who immigrated from Poland to America in the 1920s. I do not know if the story is factual, nor do I have reason to doubt it.

When she was fourteen, Tekla's family betrothed her to a 60-year-old man whose previous wife had died, leaving him with children to raise. My auntie said the man was ugly, with hair sprouting from his warts. I hardly needed that detail to understand my grandmother's horror at the prospect of marrying someone forty-plus years her senior.

Tekla ran away to Częstochowa, to the Jasna Góra Monastery, where a famous Black Madonna is housed. She went to pray for deliverance from her fate.

Her family found her and brought her back to southern Poland, deep in the Carpathian Mountains, to face her arranged marriage. She ran away again. Her parents were distressed—she was defying their dictates, bringing shame to the family— and did the only thing they could think of: they arranged her passage with a friend on a boat to America.

I wonder what it was like for her to land at Ellis Island, a young girl alone in an enormous, teeming city so unlike her mountain village. She eventually met a man, Albert, and married in Detroit, Michigan. I sensed she loved him, and he her, though both had volatile personalities. They birthed twelve children; eleven lived to adulthood.

Tillie cleaned houses to help support the family. Her husband worked as a school custodian. She did not assimilate easily and refused to speak English. My relationship with her was not based on words—it was rooted in a feeling. A feeling of being loved.

She never lost her devotion to the Black Madonna, Our Lady of Częstochowa.

It was Christmas Eve, 1963. I stood, a red-headed ten-year-old, with my back pressed against Grandma's flour-smudged apron. Her generous arms encircled me as we gazed together at the image of the Black Madonna on the living room wall. The only light came from the colored bulbs on the Christmas tree. Faint scents of kielbasa, gołąbki, and pierogi lingered in the air.

I felt an enchanted energy pass between my grandmother and the Lady—devotion, trust, love, sorrow. Grandma spoke to me in Polish. I could not understand her words, but I felt her reverence.

I vowed to one day visit the Black Madonna. I kept that promise.

That moment lit the flame of my lifelong fascination with the Divine Feminine. I searched for her in conversations with nuns at my all-girls Catholic high school, in university courses on world religions, and in indigenous spiritual experiences. The more I learned—especially about the Dark Goddess archetype—the more awe I felt for what she has symbolized through the ages: the dark womb from which all things emerge, the source of our common origin and oneness, and of our diversity. The depths of sorrow and joy. The emptying out that comes with grief, and the creativity of transformative rebirth. Compassion born from suffering.

Over time, I came to know the Lady as a mysterious yet intimately felt presence—an empathy found in stillness. She became the loving container of my sorrows, holding when I needed to set them aside to manage the demands of daily life. She became an alchemical force, transforming pain into resilience and strength. She became a metaphor for the crucible of creativity.

I now know her as the ground zero of my life. She is a comforter; she is a provocateur. She is feminine, she is a mother. She is understanding; she is the unknown. She is warm joy; she is cold no-nonsense courage. She is me, and I am her. It is she I long to BE. I know her as Love.

We live in a world where many use their hatchets—words, money, and power—against women, children, marginalized people, the poor, immigrants, the LGBTQ+ community, public education, universities, and the old and sick. I ask myself: what is there to do?

I have read enough to know that what is happening in the world is the result of decades of organizing, backed by dark, dark money, and often conducted in the name of God by some religious institutions – including, extremist factions within the Catholic Church in which I was raised. Their motivations have little in common with the Christ Consciousness, the heart imbued in social justice, that Jesus emulated in human form.

Like my grandmother, I find myself on a metaphorical pilgrimage to the Black Madonna. For me, prayer is listening within. I wait quietly for the thoughts that guide me, for the inner whisper of the next right step, for understanding. For intuitive nudges. When I feel comforted, and grounded—I act. And yet, I know the most powerful contribution I can make is to BE the essence of the Black Madonna: loving, compassionate, and empathic. But also, to CREATE from those states.

We are all vulnerable to victimization, a deep sense of grievance, bitterness, intolerance, or hatred. For some individuals, this has become an identity, even a politic.

My descents into the loving compassion of the Black Madonna, the Dark Goddess, remind me that if I join that energy of bitterness and grievance, I become it. If I stay in love and forgiveness, I create more of it.

In her book *The Four Sacred Gifts*, Dr. Anita Sanchez shares that in 1994, twenty-seven Indigenous elders from around the world came together and named four sacred gifts that could soften even the hardest heart and transform our world. The one that struck deepest in me was the first: "Forgive the unforgivable." That is what it will take to move beyond any bitterness and grievance so we can receive the other gifts: healing, unity, and hope in action.

Hope in Action. Our creative power. The energy of the Dark Goddess is peace-loving, but it is not passive.

I suspect that over time, my grandmother forgave her family. I believe she embodied hope in action by creating and loving her own family—including me—here in America.

I await inner guidance to create in any way I can, grounded in Hope in Action. As I muse in *Initiation*:

> *"You wanted immunity*
> *from Life's assaults.*
> *But I knew,*
> *every delay suspended you*
> *in a world of make-believe,*
> *a world of stunted consciousness.*
>
> *Your initiation to harsh reality*
> *hid a boon,*
> *a gem,*
> *a diamond,*

*the brilliance of seeing,
the brilliance of hearing,
the brilliance of knowing,
the brilliance of Love…*

*One day when least expected,
you will awaken from dreamtime slumber
and look up to see my face.
My ebony skin glows.
My magnificent candle bounces fire into your eyes.
You will know
that I never left you.
We are forged and fused
in the inferno of unquenchable love."*

In his work, *Turning Point*, Rilke reminds us, *"The work of the eyes is done. Go now and do the heart-work on the images imprisoned within you."*

While we move through any heart of darkness, may the courageous will of a mother's love and her essential creativity reflect into our eyes and guide us toward justice, humanitarian action, well-being, and transformative, unquenchable love.

Connect with Linda Sandel Pettit

Thank you for reading *Elegies to a Dark Goddess*. I hope in some small way that the poems stirred your soul and touched your story. Please leave a review on the reading platform of your choice. Doing so helps other readers find terrific books and spreads the message of transcendence at the heart of the book.

Follow me on Substack at: https://substack.com/@drlmsp

Follow me on Bluesky at: https://bsky.app/profile/lmspettit.bsky.social

Follow me on Linked In at: https://www.linkedin.com/in/linda-sandel-pettit/

For more about my books, events, and services, and to read my blog or sign up for my mailing list, please visit https://drlindapettit.com

Book me to speak at: https://drlindapettit.com/book-dr-linda-to-speak/

Leave a message at: https://drlindapettit.com/contact. These messages arrive directly in my inbox, and I love hearing from my community of readers.

About the Author

With keen intuition and a gift for seeing the unseen, Dr. Linda **Sandel Pettit** helps courageous intuitive, creative women master their magic—so they can leave legacies of leadership, creative self-expression, and a life lived fully.

Drawing on decades of experience as a psychologist, writer, and spiritual mentor, Linda supports women in unlocking their inner wisdom and creating from it with grace, purpose, and power. She points to the essence of spiritual consciousness: the sacred capacity to create again and again from the deep well of intuitive knowing—the formless intelligence of Mind, the presence of Love, and the spiritual artistry of Thought.

Her coaching sanctuary, **Master Your Magic!**, is a circle of transformation where women come home to their true voices, strengthen their intuitive trust, and claim their place as visionary leaders, creators, and healers. Learn more at https://drlindapettit.com.

Linda holds a doctorate in counseling psychology from West Virginia University (1991), a master's in counselor education from Siena Heights University (1983), and a bachelor's in journalism from Michigan State University.

She shares a life of love and exploration with her husband, Bill Pettit, MD, a psychiatrist, and internationally recognized influencer at the intersection of spirituality, medicine, neuroscience, and psychiatry. The "pair of docs" live in Phoenix, Arizona, and are over-the-moon about their large, blended family: five children and their partners, eleven grandchildren, and three great-grandchildren.

Linda finds joy in cycling, swimming, walking, reading, writing, and savoring a great cup of coffee.

Linda's Writing

Leaning into Curves: Trusting the Wild, Intuitive Way of Love, IW Press

A self-help memoir written for all the poets, pirates and lovers who have never quite fitted in, who have wondered who and what God is, who have always known there was magic inside them wanting to be free and who have felt the despair of lost love, human suffering, tragic mistakes, and earth-shaking grief.

It is FACT that if you know where to look, LOVE is guiding you through all of it ... one thought, one intuitive knowing, one mystical synchronicity and one heartbeat at a time. LOVE only asks that you LISTEN, TRUST, and LOOK always for BEAUTY. Do not wait another minute to SEE the intuitive way of LOVE unfolding in YOUR life.

Praise for Leaning into Curves:

"Linda Sandel Pettit has walked the walk, ridden the wild ride, and ... come back ... to bring us wisdom, insights, and hope. A page turner from the first page to the last..."
—Michael Pastore, Zorba Editing

"... A book to laugh with, cry with, and feel your soul resonate to ... healing and extraordinary."
—Nicci Attfield, Reviewer, Reedsy Discovery

Stories from the Muses: Become A Better Writer [Method Writing with Jules Swales - Book 2] IW Press

Archetypal Muses have influenced art for generations. In Jack Grapes Method Writing taught by Jules Swales, there is a level called Disquieting Muses devoted to writing from the seven muses. Readers will experience fifteen writers, including Linda Sandel Pettit, who discover themselves and become better writers through muse inspiration.

Praise for Stories from the Muses:

"Powerful. Thought provoking. Important. Every line is a winner. I've never heard of a book like this, and the whole concept is so interesting! I loved every word!"
    —Nancy Aronie, NPR Commentator, Author, Columnist.

Acknowledgements

I would not have written *Elegies to a Dark Goddess* had I not been challenged to explore my inner poet by my Writing Teacher, Author and Poet, Jules Swales. The classes she teaches in the Method Writing of Jack Grapes are my creative community. She and the writers in her community have challenged and inspired me not only to hone my writer's voice but also to live from my deep truth. I am eternally grateful.

Publishing and promoting a book is a thicket of challenges! My Publisher, Maria Iliffe-Wood, of IW Press, is a steady and knowledgeable author and guide whose faith in my writing encourages me always. Thank you!

A special thank you to Renuka Susan O'Connell, Author, Poet, and Artist, who read one of the first *Elegies to a Dark Goddess* and created the artwork for the cover. What a gift! Your kindness and artistic gifts enrich my life.

Thank you to my beta readers, Patsy Kisner, Anni Silverdale Poole, Doris Boyle, and Sarah Hook Nilsson, for the gift of your time and your honest feedback.

My first creativity coach, Gail McMeekin [find her at https://gailmcmeekin.com] deserves a special and heartfelt nod. Had I not read her book, *The Twelve Secrets of Highly Creative Women: A Portable Mentor* and worked with her when coaching was brand new, it might have taken much longer for me to master my own magic.

The beautiful continuous line drawings within this book were licensed from the istockphoto.com collection. A heartfelt thank you to the artists: mitay20 (illustrating *The Right to Be*), Mariia Klymenko (illustrating *Crazy Love*), Tanya Syrytsyna (illustrating *Messages from the Black Madonna*), and kiyanochka (illustrating *Yearning*). Each of these artists are Ukranian; taylan_ozgur (illustrating *Mystery*) is in the UK.

I am deeply grateful to proofreader/editor, Michael Pastore, who went far beyond catching typos to suggesting substantive changes that polished to a shine the power of the poetry. Find him at: https://zorbapress.com/authors/michael-pastore/.

My heartfelt thanks to Catherine Williams for her artistic interior formatting and patience with my adjustments. And I am grateful to Iain Hill, for a perfect cover design and prompt responsiveness to numerous tweaks! While both of you work behind-the-scenes, your artistic touches add immeasurably to the book's poetic look and feel.

A special thank you to all of the people who form the rich tapestry of my world—these elegies are born of our shared exploration of the mystery of life.

And to you, Bill Pettit, for your unfailing support of my creative life.

Of course, *Elegies to a Dark Goddess* would not have taken form without Rainer Maria Rilke's sharing of his gifts via rich, evocative, transcendent poetry. Amen. Hallelujah.

Book Circle Questions

1. **Exploring the Dark Goddess:** The book engages deeply with the figure of the Black Madonna as a symbol of transformation, sorrow, and love. How did your perception of the Dark Goddess evolve as you read?

2. **Personal Initiation:** The first elegy, *Initiation*, describes a harrowing descent into the abyss. Did you experience a personal "initiation" into wisdom through loss or hardship in childhood or adolescence? How did it shape you?

3. **Free Will vs. Destiny:** In *Free Will*, the poet wrestles with the tension between personal choice and divine orchestration. Do you believe in destiny, free will, or an interplay between the two? How does the book challenge or affirm your beliefs?

4. **The Alchemy of Grief:** The elegies explore the transformation of grief into wisdom. How did the book change the way you view loss and sorrow? Did any passage particularly resonate with your own experiences?

5. **The Power of Storytelling:** The *Epilogue* reflects on how the author's Polish grandmother's faith and the mystery of the Black Madonna shaped her spiritual journey. Are there figures in your life who have influenced your spiritual or personal growth in similar ways?

6. **Yearning and Surrender:** In *Yearning*, the poet speaks of a restless longing that only finds resolution in surrender to the present moment. How do you relate to this theme? Have you experienced a moment of deep surrender in your own life?

7. **Integration into Life:** If you were to write your own Elegies, what would you lament about your life? Celebrate? Honor more?

www.ingramcontent.com/pod-product-compliance
Ingram Content Group UK Ltd.
Pitfield, Milton Keynes, MK11 3LW, UK
UKHW022315290825

462348UK00006B/12